My Stupid CEO

SIDNEY S. PRASAD

ISBN: 192767624X
ISBN-13: 978-1-927676-24-0

DEDICATION

This book is dedicated to my special friend Gursharn, who motivated me to write some trashy novels while ratting on the business world. Thank you for your words of wisdom and eternal gift of friendship!

CONTENTS

ACKNOWLEDGMENTS

If one were to Google the word "stupid," chances are they would see a picture of My Stupid CEO. The definition of "stupid," as we know, refers to a dense being. However, there are certain entities where this term could be expanded on. Some people may feel that anyone who is not at par with their IQ level is stupid. Others may use the word "stupid" to describe someone's actions.

In the business world, CEO is the abbreviation for *Chief Executive Officer*. The title "CEO" carries the highest amount of prestige and honor. The buck ideally stops at the CEO's suite, as the CEO is more or less the heartbeat of the company. The entire future of the corporation and its employees ride on the CEO's shoulders.

In a perfect world, one could assume that the Powers that Be would assign this position to an intellectually sophisticated individual. It only makes sense to entrust the savviest, most erudite person to manage an entity and all its components for the stakeholders, right? To simplify this, the manager of a ritzy burger joint should be knowledgeable of the methodology involved in tossing the fries along with the flipping of the burgers. If we were to graduate to the executive level, then a CEO should have a fairly broad knowledge base of human resources, marketing strategies, up-to-date accounting standards, logistics, and overall operations of the entire company.

Unfortunately, there are the odd exceptions where a company appears to be doing great on an economic scale but the lackluster leadership is equivalent to a fourth-grader managing the sandbox during recess. Believe it or not, there are companies whose directors carry the CEO's dead weight, which sits at the top of the pyramid. But like attracts like, and sometimes it's not only the CEO who gets a free ride; its middle managers or directors get carried as well by the sales staff and junior executives. The front-line employees ultimately end up becoming the backbone of the company.

I truly believe that when it comes to success, there are only two types of individuals. The first type encompasses people who have arrived at their level of fame and fortune from hard work and intelligence. The second category involves people who have coasted through life and achieved the greatest piece of the American dream by fluke.

This book revolves around My Stupid CEO, whose name is Izzy Cumming. Not only is he an imbecile, but his legacy is based on confusion and controversy. Everyone in the business world, including my colleagues and myself, has always pondered how such a bonehead could get so freaking successful. Prepare to get entertained by a tale about *My Stupid CEO*!

Disclaimer: All characters in this book are imaginary. Resemblances to any person living or dead are purely coincidental.

1 DECEPTION

Countless business school graduates share the same childhood story. While playing with our Lego watching the daily soap operas with our mothers, we became intrigued with the way business figures were portrayed on the big screen: their expensive suits, luxury offices, beautiful secretaries, lavish lunches, business trips, and golden parachutes. All of us held onto those pictures of fictional figures such as Jack Abbott and Victor Newman from *The Young and the Restless* and strove to become like them one day, or at least work for someone brilliant who closely resembled them. We worked our asses off to get into the best business schools and didn't leave until we'd earned the letters M.B.A. to place on our business cards. Finally, we were ready to enter the corporate world, anticipating that there would be a bidding war for securing our talents.

Reality kicks in when we make the astonishing discovery that the marketplace is saturated with MBAs and we are a dime a dozen. A large portion of us end up going back to school to legitimately hide out in shame. A few of us end up driving a cab or pouring coffee at Starbucks. Some MBA grads end up jobless and penniless for a few years, regretting not playing it safe and getting government jobs. Then, there is a small portion of our flock that actually get the opportunity to break into the business world.

"My Stupid CEO broke into a greenhouse to see what was inside."

—Sidney S. Prasad

As we are directed to our offices on our first day of work, we learn that we have to share it with another twenty people. For privacy, we are furnished with cloth walls, otherwise known as a cubicle. We do get the luxury of being allowed to sit underneath our desks for those really important calls that we need to focus on. Rather than getting a well-deserved executive position, we end up with one of the following titles: sales executive, account manager, marketing coordinator, or consultant. The six-figure salary we banked on is reduced to thirty thousand dollars per year. The beautiful, busty, blonde secretary that we envisioned does not exist; she was replaced with electronic voice mail. The big executive decisions that we were hoping to consult on entail ordering lunch for the directors and warming their vehicles for them during winter. We don't get time to model our expensive second-hand suits because we're too busy phoning random people and convincing them to buy shit that they don't need.

Just to make our office life complete, we soon find out that we have to report to a bipolar manager. In these sort of work environments, only the *crème de la crème* of psychotics get the opportunity of making our lives hell. I'm sure everyone out there has worked for crazy nutjob managers. But the ones in the business world need to be locked up in a mental asylum and examined by not just one, but a team of psychiatrists.

"My Stupid CEO thought his mom's sisters lived on an ant farm."

—Sidney S. Prasad

To complete this picture, we are forced to work in the most hostile environment ever imagined with a bunch people who are beneath us. The personality types range from the office pothead to the office slut and, of course, the Negative Nelly that whines about every freaking thing before it happens. The shitty thing about the grown-up workplace is that it's just like elementary school, where we were stuck sharing a classroom with a bunch of losers for eight hours a day.

"My Stupid CEO thought a Porsche 911 was a police car."

—Sidney S. Prasad

Initially when we got hired, our thoughts were filled with gratitude and thankfulness. We were grateful to our employers for getting us out of the cold and helping us get a foot into the business world. With the record high level of unemployment and poverty, it's a cruel world for some people. It's quite sad that there are many people appearing to be homeless and living on the streets. In fact, if one were to observe a beggar on the street, they would agree that only two things happen when someone passes by them. Either they completely ignore the beggar, or they donate some money or food to the needy individual. I worked at a downtown restaurant as a busboy during high school and made a shocking discovery. There were a group of punk rockers that used to panhandle in front of the restaurant for a few hours a day. Later, they would come into the restaurant and pay for their meals with platinum credit cards. This really intrigued me because their appearance would make the average person conclude that they were destitute, and maybe even homeless.

I purposely went out of my way to give extra-special service to the group of panhandling punk rockers to find out the logic behind their actions. After I befriended them, they disclosed to me that they were from upper middle class families on the socioeconomic scale. They even admitted to residing in luxurious apartments on the west side of town. Almost everyone in their group was in their third year of university, and they found that it was easier to beg than to work. The panhandling punk rockers laughed at everyone who was stupid enough to assist them in maintaining their lifestyle. They averaged out about one hundred to two hundred per day with their hands out.

"My Stupid CEO thought a serial killer ruined his breakfast."

—Sidney S. Prasad

I would feel bamboozled if I were one of the idiots who got conned by those punks. But thankfully, I held on tight to my hard-earned five dollar per hour paycheck and spent it at the nudie bar instead.

I'm confident that you have witnessed the scenario of an extremely well-dressed man going into a bank and starting to scream at the teller. The justification for his anger is that the bank closed his account, which was in overdraft. On the same token, I'm sure you have also seen some grubby-looking tradesman walk into the bank with grease and shit all over his coveralls. The funny thing is the tradesman pulled out a big wad of one hundred dollar bills and made a deposit without flinching.

Life is very deceptive and manipulative, because sometimes things end up being completely the opposite after we investigate. Prior to accepting this job working for My Stupid CEO, I did major research, which led me to believe that he was a brilliant man. There were countless positive write-ups on his business successes. His official company website boasted about his company having a five thousand percent increase in business over the last ten years. I had seen his name affiliated with some top charities as well, and I thought I found my future mentor. Like many business school graduates, I was willing to work for a shitty poverty-level wage to learn from the best. I also thought I'd take advantage of the company Rolodex and rub my elbows with the cream of the crop in the business world. This experience alone would be like becoming The Apprentice.

"My Stupid CEO attempted to install a fireplace inside an igloo."

—Sidney S. Prasad

Boy, was I wrong; I would have done better using one of the panhandling punk rockers as my mentor. Not only did I waste my time and energy working for this asshole, I also got exposed to how dirty the business world really was. My Stupid CEO, Izzy Cumming, was the dumbest, dirtiest, and cheapest idiot I have ever encountered. The media at times slams incompetent business and world leaders for their stupidity, but this guy took the crown. There was utterly no rationality in his business decisions, and his success was based on pure fluke. I am still plagued by the question of how he made it to the CEO's suite. Whenever I see a replica Lamborghini, a fake Rolex watch, or a knockoff Gucci handbag, I am reminded that life is deceptive!

"When his business tanked, My Stupid CEO tried to commit suicide by jumping out of the basement window."

—Sidney S. Prasad

2 HOW HE GOT RICH

I The company that My Stupid CEO represented was a typical dot-com business that sold janitorial supplies on the Internet. I was hired as an account executive as a reward for my extensive business background. I figured this job would be a piece of cake, considering that I was officially the most educated person in this company. I speculated that it would take me about one year to get promoted into a director's position. My formula for success consisted of the following: hard work, self motivation, goal orientation, backbiting, and intensive ass-kissing.

The first critical thing on my agenda was to interview My Stupid CEO and learn about his victories on the previous boards that he served on. I was expecting for him to tell me stories about taking a company public and earning the shareholders millions of dollars on the IPO. Or a tale about a time when he turned around a sinking company that was in the red and took it back up into positive green territory. Guess what? Apparently, the fucker never had a job in his entire life!

"How the fuck was that possible," I thought. I got my first job when I was eleven years old, handing out flyers and pissing on people's lawns. I had to wash dishes and flip pizzas all through junior high and high school while this fucker had his thumb up his ass.

"My Stupid CEO thought a branch manager was a lumberjack."

—Sidney S. Prasad

I was really curious now how he made his first dollar, as that's a pretty standard question I ask of all self-made millionaires. He told me that he used to pick up soda cans and bottles out of dumpsters all through high school. Obviously, this guy never got laid in high school, jumping into people's garbage like he was Oscar the Grouch. In my mind, I knew there were not enough empty pop bottles in North America for seed money to start a company that large. My Stupid CEO Izzy Cumming told me that after high school, he turned into a creeper. He basically would stand in the parking lot of Costco and offer to deliver people's shit for them at a small price in his pickup truck. After years of frugality and saving all his pennies, he started a business of purchasing janitorial supplies and reselling them at a premium price. The justification for charging roughly thirty to one hundred percent markup was reflected through next-day delivery service.

After hearing his story, I was convinced that there were a lot more stupid people in my city than met the eye. I personally couldn't justify paying double the price for some paper towels because they got delivered the next day. I started to realize why there were so many morbidly obese secretaries in my vicinity. In all my previous gigs, the receptionist would have to take her lunch break on the road while picking up our toilet paper and supplies. My Stupid CEO would basically con businesses into buying into the phrase, "time is money." He would then twist the arms of the supporting workers and ask them if they would want to run to the store and pick up shit during a snowstorm. Apparently, those two questions built his company into ten million dollars in annual sales.

"My Stupid CEO locked himself out of his convertible car while the top was down."

—Sidney S. Prasad

Calculating some rough figures in my head, I couldn't figure out how he kept his operational budget low enough to make this company profitable. I asked Izzy Cumming how he found the space to store the one hundred thousand different items listed in the catalogue. He told me to take a walk and accompany him to the warehouse. This is where I learned how dirty and crafty the corporate world really was. My Stupid CEO only stocked a few hundred of the most avidly used items. He told me that every afternoon, he sends out a truck to various wholesale warehouses to purchase the products and drop them off at his warehouse. His warehouse staff would rip the price tags off and reload the goods into boxes with his company logo marked on them. He said that under no circumstances were the account executives allowed to tip off their clients that they were pulling this shit behind the scenes. He instructed the account executives to always give their clients the impression that the company owned several warehouses that they pulled stock from.

I noticed a bunch of bite-size Halloween candy bars on the ground, and My Stupid CEO told me they were incentives for the clients. Basically, if someone spent one hundred dollars, they would get one a bite-size chocolate bar, a sponge, or a bar of soap. If the client spent two hundred, they would get two items, and if they spent three hundred, they would get three items, and then they were cut off from freebies. This was plain outright absurd on My Stupid CEO's part. Why not give a whole fucking chocolate bar as an incentive instead of embarrassing the company? Not only was Izzy Cumming a dummy head, but he was a cheap shit too!

"My Stupid CEO got banned from Las Vegas for shitting on the craps table."

—Sidney S. Prasad

Okay, so the company was making decent margin on their products and saving a ton of money on warehousing costs. However, there was still a piece of the puzzle missing to make the overall financial statement balance out.

We walked out of the warehouse and past the purchasing department, and I got introduced to the two ladies who spearheaded that department. Pu Ping, a middle-aged Asian female, was the head purchaser. Winnie Bago, who roughly weighed five-hundred pounds, was the other purchaser. She had some Guess? jeans on; I guessed size forty-five. I bet if she went on a diet, she could solve the world hunger problem in a jiffy.

I overhead Winnie Bago negotiating for some cleaning supplies while munching on a jelly doughnut. I was amazed at how anyone would negotiate while eating, especially in the presence of their boss. My Stupid CEO explained that some of our local suppliers would periodically call and offer almost-expired cleaning supplies at a deep discount. That's why he didn't care if Winnie Bago was swallowing a buffet or two while negotiating.

I questioned the three-hundred-sixty-five day hassle-free company return policy, because I could certainly imagine a ton of angry clients pissed off about expired bleach or furniture polish. My Stupid CEO responded that the client only gets one week to return any liquid or solid cleaning supplies. Not only was Izzy Cumming a crook, but a really dumb one. There is absolutely no way he could keep up this ordeal, screwing people long-term on expired toilet bowl cleaner.

"My Stupid CEO thought attorneys wore lawsuits."

—Sidney S. Prasad

I decided to get technical on this creep and question the two-year warranty on buffers and mechanical soap dispensers. My Stupid CEO explained to me that those things break down all the time, and we only had the client's back for the first ninety days. He said after that, we kindly Google the 1-800 phone number of the manufacturer and pass the buck to them. I reflected on the last six years of business school I spent learning about ethics and morals. I was flabbergasted that this creep was one of the captains of industry representing corporate America. Maybe I should have taken the job selling timeshares in Compton instead. At least that way I wouldn't have to worry about the return policy, because the client would probably die from a drive-by shooting ten days after the purchase.

Something clicked in my mind as I remembered where I first seen My Stupid CEO. He was on a national charity telethon the year before, as a host. If I weren't so desperate for a job, I would have ratted him out. But I really needed the money to pay off some indecent exposure fines and legal fees. I commended My Stupid CEO for his charity efforts and asked him if his company ever donated to their client's grassroots events. His response utterly disgusted me, as he really reaffirmed his stupidity and short-term thinking. Basically, he instructs his account executives to explain to their clients that their donation and gift requests will be passed to a panel of board members to review. After the client is approved, a gift will be disbursed. The gifts consisted of an empty cooler, a dollar-store barbecue tool set, or a jar of candy. Here's the kicker: The client would only receive their donation gift if it were attached to an order. My Stupid CEO said this was his methodology in squeezing an extra hundred out of his clients.

"My Stupid CEO needed an hour to cook Minute Rice."

—Sidney S. Prasad

As the way the universe unfolds, there was no way this thief could get away with being such a con artist without someone ripping him off as well. I positioned my next question on trouble areas of the company. My Stupid CEO told me that he speculated that he was getting ripped off by a foreign web design team in Yemen. He admitted to giving them over a million over the last year, but for some reason, they couldn't create a website for him to sell internationally. I instantly smiled inside as I pictured some nerdy computer geeks floating around in a pool of champagne with the money My Stupid CEO was paying them. In his twisted little mind, My Stupid CEO was confident in expanding his business internationally and pissing off the global community.

With the shenanigans Izzy Cummings was pulling, I figured he would have a large army of outside salespeople backing him up. Surprisingly enough, his entire outside sales force consisted of two people. Hank E. Panky and Wilma Dickfit were solely in charge of increasing the company's market share for the whole metropolitan area. Any amateur CEO would have assigned at least twenty salespeople for such a large terrain. Wilma Dickfit was a great ambassador to the organization; she was outspoken, well dressed, and beautiful. Hank E. Panky looked like Colonel Sanders, with his wrinkled white blazer and black bow tie. Quite frankly, Hank E. Panky should have auditioned for the part of Tattoo on *Fantasy Island*.

"Are there sex addicts in the Virgin Islands?"

—Sidney S. Prasad, *Don't Ask Dumb Questions!*

3 WINNERS CLUB

A long time ago, some well-known authors approached a peak performance coach and complained that they were sick of earning incomes in the ten-million to thirty-million range. Their goal was to increase their income to one hundred million per year. The peak performance coach requested that they evaluate their reference group and their incomes. Basically, you list the six people you associate with the most and then list their incomes next to their names. Once you total all the incomes and divide by six, then your income would be that average. The peak performance coach instructed the gentlemen to hang out only with people in the one hundred million per year bracket or higher, and they would see significant increases in their income. They took his advice and saw their earnings skyrocket. We can apply this advice to our own lives as well.

"My Stupid CEO thought the Grim Reaper got around on the Soul Train."

—Sidney S. Prasad

One could assume, based on My Stupid CEO's earnings track record, he would have some brilliant, savvy people working for him. His executive team consisted of himself and his wife Anita Dyck, who sucked her way into a vice president's position. Anita Dyck started as an employee but pulled a White House intern scam and used her oral talents to move up the ranks. She purposely got herself pregnant and made My Stupid CEO surrender half the company to her in exchange for marriage and a lifetime of bad sex. She was dumber than a doorknob and locked herself in the toilet one day and pissed herself. The last executive team member was Hugh Jass, the company's beloved CFO. He was pretty much the brains of the operation and served over a decade carrying My Stupid CEO's dumb ass.

"You tell your kids not to talk to strangers, yet you let them answer the telephone."

—Sidney S. Prasad, *Telemarketer's Revenge: The Customer Is Always Wrong, Bitch!*

With the exception of Hugh Jass, there wasn't too much intellectual horsepower on the executive team, so I presumed the middle managers would be a tad bit sharper. Pu Ping, the purchasing manager, was stolen away from the competition. She was the type of person who needed two hours to watch *60 Minutes*. She did have a brain, but was too overworked to access it. Her department was notorious for over-promising and under-delivering. There were times when she would forget to order condiments for the company break room and we would have to go looting at McDonald's.

The logistical department, which was a complete disaster, was headed by Ray Pist. He had been with the company for decades and should have been locked up in a mental asylum a long time ago. He was the kind of fuckhead that would give paragraph-long answers for simple questions. For instance, if you asked him for a user care manual for a buffer, he would respond like this: "I can absolutely furnish you with the necessary documentation that you require to facilitate your technical needs." Just a simple "yes" or "no" would do, wouldn't you agree?

Rumor had it that Ray Pist used to be an elementary school teacher, but got fired for being an asshole. I wouldn't be surprised if it was a day-care that he got fired from for doing something creepy. I could picture this fucker taking his dates to Chuck E. Cheese.

"My Stupid CEO was curious as to what time 7-11 closed."

—Sidney S. Prasad

The biggest thorn on the company was My Bipolar Manager, Iman S. Hole. The entire company unanimously agreed that one of the worst moves My Stupid CEO made was to hire this moron. My Bipolar Manager was a plague and a virus, whichever one you consider worse. Almost every workplace has one of these idiots.

My Bipolar Manager was the kind of guy that would rip a strip off his employees and then five minutes later ask them out for a drink and act like nothing happened. There aren't enough negative words in the dictionary to describe the behavior of this jerkoff. At times we would refer to him as a Nazi because he was so power-hungry and got a kick out of making our lives miserable. My Bipolar Manager Iman S. Hole was famous for assigning a specific task and then completely forgetting that he barked that order. This would lead him to taking one of his employees into the boardroom and pissing on them for an hour about going over his bald head. The only way to alleviate the situation was to always print out any emailed assignment from him and keep it within arm's reach to counter his Nazi attacks.

"My Stupid CEO thought shoemakers made booty calls."

—Sidney S. Prasad

The entire company hated My Bipolar Manager. I wrote an entire book about this boob for anyone interested in learning about managers who need to get their heads checked. My Bipolar Manager was really insecure and a loser. He had a weird funky disease in which he would steal a person's idea and take credit for it like it was his own.

My Bipolar Manager Iman S. Hole was threatened by older, sophisticated females. We had a sales superstar on our team of account executives; her name was Beverly Hill. She was a reformed crack addict who had turned her life around. She was so brilliant that she managed fifty percent of the company's accounts and still had time to mentor people. It only took three months for My Bipolar Manager Iman S. Hole to drive her back to the crack house and make her quit her job. That should have been a red flag to My Stupid CEO, but unfortunately, it just flew over his head.

"My Bipolar Manager is the only guy in the world that gets angry when eating a Happy Meal."

—Sidney S. Prasad, *My Bipolar Manager*

My Bipolar Manager replaced Beverly Hill with Yora Hogg and Sheeza Freak. No CEO with a second-grade education would find it economically feasible to replace one person with two and pay double the salary. Yora Hogg was a younger female, but quite mature for her age. Her personality only went two ways: She either loved you or hated you. Thankfully, I was in her good books and we never pissed each other off. She had the Wild Kingdom theme at her place, with a collection of cats, dogs, snakes, and birds.

Sheeza Freak was in her mid-twenties and really down to earth. I give her props for playing politics well and never becoming an enemy of anyone. She had a weird obsession with Volkswagens and Starbucks, and I could totally see her being a spokesperson for either company. Initially, she was My Bipolar Manager's and My Stupid CEO's pet, and none of us had an issue with this at all.

"If we are what we eat, then my boss must be a carnivore, because he is the biggest meathead!"

—Sidney S. Prasad, *My Bipolar Manager*

Eileen Dover was also part of the sales team. She was known as the office Debbie Downer. Fuck, this chick could never be happy, and she always had something to bitch about. Our desks were next to each other and I got stuck hearing her rant about the most miniscule things. Like, she would even get choked up at the soda pop factories for changing the taste of Coke. Buy fucking Coca-Cola Classic and solve your problem.

Between her and My Stupid CEO, I'm not sure who was more stupid. She worked in the exact same position for over seven years with no promotion. I figured after flipping burgers for a few years, one would want to master the art of tossing the fries and learn a new skill. My Stupid CEO should have created a special position for someone who had dedicated such a big portion of their life to his company.

"My Stupid CEO wore his swimming trunks to the pool hall."

—Sidney S. Prasad

My other colleague on the sales team was Liz Bien, who was the office slut. She served as an informant to My Bipolar Manager and constantly leaked information about us. This chick was a chronic, pathological liar and got away with murder. On her second day of work, she claimed that her house was robbed and couldn't make it to work. Five minutes after getting excused from work we found her on Facebook contributing to her fetish forum.

Sharon Needles was another self-proclaimed ex-drug-addict who My Stupid CEO recruited prior to my arrival. I'm not sure how he paid her, in crack or in actual currency. Sharon Needles looked like Austin Powers and was always thumping around like a jackass. Her personality type involved being a yes-woman. Basically, she was the company android and would do whatever she was asked. She actually made less than me, despite three years more seniority.

There were a couple more idiots who were part of My Stupid CEO's dream team, who I will touch on later. The company had roughly forty employees, and pretty much everyone had some sort of addiction, crisis, or severe personal issue. I couldn't see any of my colleagues being contestants in a beauty pageant. My Stupid CEO scared half our clients away by flamboyantly displaying all of his mutant employees' pictures on the company website. I was the only one who got away without a picture. I was embarrassed to be associated with this brat pack advertised on the World Wide Web.

"My Stupid CEO thought proctologists and crack addicts were the same."

—Sidney S. Prasad

4 COMPENSATION

My father always preached to me about the security of a
government job. His philosophy was, serve your country
for twenty-five years, and your country will pay you back
with a secured pension. I could appreciate how he arrived
at this hypothesis. Believe it or not, in my eyes, Canada is a
backward country in some aspects. The salary for a
university professor starts off in the sixty-five thousand to
seventy-five thousand dollars per year range. The starting
salary for a typical policeman is roughly in the fifty
thousand range. However, after four years on the force,
the police officer's salary would rise to seventy-five
thousand dollars. The university professor needs a PhD to
get his ass a teaching job at the university, while the law
enforcement official only requires a GED (Good Enough
Diploma), a CPR license and a First Aid Certificate.
Basically, the minimum requirement involves screwing a
CPR dummy every few years to keep the license valid and
a dog-shit high-school diploma, while the poor professor is
stuck sweating off his ass for eight years in university.

From an early age, I was attracted to the corporate lifestyle with its many perks. There are countless stories about business executives who were awarded millions of dollars in compensation, stock options, and golden parachutes for their efforts. I figured a couple of degrees in business would land me a dream job that would allow me to run circles around the civil servants and professors. I was confident that I was destined for success and would become a business icon one day.

"My Stupid CEO thought the wind had a blow job."

—Sidney S. Prasad

Entering a well known and profitable company, I was expecting that My Stupid CEO would be throwing crazy money at me in order to keep me away from the competition. Well, life is deceptive, and my executive wage was almost half what a typical cop made.

Izzy Cumming confidently explained to me that my pay structure included a whopping thirty thousand per year in salary and commission. I was a career salesman, and knew I could make the other half of my salary up in commission. I asked him, hypothetically, if I were to bring the company one to two million dollars in sales, what type of bonus I should expect. He told me that one million dollars would earn me three thousand, and the second million would earn me an additional fifteen hundred. Our economy was in shambles, and there weren't too many options at this point. I told myself that I would excel at my position and get promoted within a year.

"Do people in Bangkok have sore dicks?"

—Sidney S. Prasad, *Don't Ask Dumb Questions!*

I was more concerned about the experience of having a millionaire mentor and learning from the best. I strongly believe that if one gets really successful at what they're doing, the money will eventually follow. But the poverty-level pay scale should have been a red flag that Izzy Cumming was a Stupid CEO. Every company where I have ever worked, the salespeople were treated like gods because they're the heartbeat of the company, securing the market share. If the salespeople don't sell, nobody eats. I thought to myself, "If I'm only going to make enough money to buy beans and bread, then what are the poor truck drivers earning?"

An inside source in the accounting department confirmed that the truck drivers were earning sixty thousand dollars a year. It didn't make any sense to me that a business school grad was earning half the amount of a grubby truck driver.

"My Stupid CEO thought *Dancing With The Stars* was a TV show about astronauts."

—Sidney S. Prasad

There are a lot of companies who compensate their employees with extra benefits. I remember reading an article back in the day about Starbucks where it was commended for being one of the only companies that gave full-time benefits to their part-time employees. There are a couple of companies that follow that model and give their employees such benefits as vision, medical, dental, stock options, etc. My Stupid CEO told me that he pays zero benefits to his employees. Well, we could sleep with his wife if we wanted to, but that would be equivalent having sex with half the company.

My Stupid CEO had another scam that he conned his employees into buying into. He would fill the staff fridge with food every ten days, and that would be the benefit plan. However, there were a lot of people living in poverty working for this cheap fuck, so on grocery day, the warehouse staff and some of the sales staff would fill their knapsacks with the food. I didn't care too much about the food, because I was fully aware of My Stupid CEO's connections with the wholesalers in getting discounted, almost-expired food and janitorial products.

Another perk My Stupid CEO initially offered was a birthday cake on each employee's birthday. I never received a cake during the time I was there because I was a vegetarian. But you figure they could have gone to a vegan bakery or humored me with a fruit cocktail or something. Then, the Powers that Be decided to trim the birthday budget and just give a cake with a dozen names on it every quarter for whoever had their birthday during that period. That gig didn't last too long, so My Stupid CEO redesigned the birthday reward to a field trip to the casino with five dollars in chips on him.

"My Stupid CEO thought that telecom employees were phony."

—Sidney S. Prasad

In addition to practically working for food, there was another bonus that we were entitled to. On an employee's anniversary of their start date, they would receive a card. Not a gift card, because that would be a dream, but a shitty computer-generated "Thank You" card with nothing inside. The card wasn't made on cardstock, but printed on one-cent dinky printer paper. Unfortunately, the card didn't come with an envelope.

The employees would also get a sweaty handshake from My Stupid CEO. He wasn't into washing his hands after using the washroom, so I didn't look forward to shaking his hand. Whenever I consult in a new office I always make a point of eavesdropping to check if I can hear water running after someone flushes. The sales environment is notorious for high-fives and handshakes.

The majority of the companies where I have been employed don't consider water a fringe benefit. The competition's benefit plan included health club memberships, free car rentals, education reimbursements, child care, and NHL season tickets. Unfortunately, they weren't hiring that point in time. My Stupid CEO would occasionally splurge and give us a raffle for movie passes to a G-rated movie. The challenge was winning the tickets and then convincing someone to join me at the awkward time the movie would be playing.

"Order your date fish and you fed her for the night. Teach her how to fish and you're not getting laid!"

—Sidney S. Prasad, *My Bipolar Manager*

My lazy relatives who worked for the government told me something in English that sounded like a foreign language to me. Apparently, the government gave them sick days, family days, and personal days on top of their six weeks of vacation. My Stupid CEO offered everyone a maximum of two weeks' vacation per year. If a person was sick while recovering from herpes, the company wouldn't pay them for it. I guess it makes perfect sense that my employee handbook was so tiny; there were no incentives to list in there.

"My Stupid CEO thought that the Rolling Stones was a landslide."

—Sidney S. Prasad

My Stupid CEO Izzy Cumming would occasionally be a Brother Teresa and throw us a bone in respect to bonuses. If he went on a lavish vacation with his slutty wife and ugly kids, he would bring back us some cheap trinkets that he picked up on the black market. The gifts included a fifty-cent pencil sharpener, cartoon stickers for adult employees, and hard candy to break your dental work.

Entrepreneurs usually embark upon owning and operating a thriving business for profit. It only seems valid to give credit where credit is due and compensate the people who are making them money, right? What made this scenario worse was My Stupid CEO was pretty open and gloated about the exact dollar amounts the sales team was earning him. Average yearly sales were in excess of ten million dollars, with an average profit margin in the thirty five percent neighborhood. An account executive who secured two million dollars in annual sales basically gave My Stupid CEO seven hundred thousand to stuff in a tranny stripper's G-string in exchange for thirty thousand in salary. I'm surprised no one had shown up to work with a trench coat and a machine gun yet.

"My Stupid CEO asked his dentist to sell him a Bluetooth."

—Sidney S. Prasad

5 WORK ENVIRONMENT

My Stupid CEO was the type of guy who would read a book about a complete different industry and try to apply its principles to his company. He would also creep on other company's workplaces and shop for ideas on how to make our work environment more dysfunctional. I have worked in the most bizarre work environments, but this company was out of this world. Words can't express how strange this company was.

My Stupid CEO had noisemakers on each of the salespeople's desk. The noisemakers were an assortment of cat toys, baby toys, and horns. Every time someone would make a sale, the salespeople had to make noise with their special designated toy. I'm not sure how I was supposed to get a prospect to take me seriously while attempting to close a ten-thousand dollar deal on the phone when they could hear some pedophile in the background squeezing a rubber ducky. If an important business figure from another company visited the office, we had to make noise with our perverted toys as well.

"My Stupid CEO made an appointment to see a psychic."

—Sidney S. Prasad

I couldn't possibly expect readers to believe me unless they witnessed it firsthand, but My Stupid CEO also had a collection of animal-head hats: a chicken hat, a dog hat, a moose hat with antlers, a cow head hat, and many even more disturbing hats. We were forced to put the hats on during the last hour of the day. His reasoning for this was that it would boost our spirits during our critical crunch time. I would never schedule a meeting with a client during this time, because I know I would blow the deal within the first two minutes after the client walked into the building during mad-hatter time.

There were special designated days that our city would encourage people to dress in a certain color to support a charity. For example, during the month of February, there was a Pink Day. Wearing an article of pink clothing symbolized that you supported the anti-bullying movement. I am totally one hundred percent in support of unique charities, especially for kids. Maybe the next generation can recruit my services in a more sane work environment. My Stupid CEO had his own special monthly days. The last Friday of every month was Pirate Day. All of us would have to wear a ridiculous pirate eye-patch and go on a chocolate coin hunt every two hours.

"My Stupid CEO attempted to get a refund on a free refill."

—Sidney S. Prasad

During our quarterly meetings, there would be occasional themes to coincide with the next quarter's goals. I'm not sure which genius on top of the totem pole was responsible for the Sesame Street theme, but one day we were forced to listen to the Sesame Street song and Ernie's Rubber Ducky song for an hour. To complete this nightmare, My Stupid CEO's wife, Anita Dyck, showed up dressed up as Ernie and passed out rubber ducks to a bunch of middle-aged adults. If anything, this deterred us from getting excited about achieving the company goals for the next quarter.

My Stupid CEO and his team of rocket scientists topped the Sesame Street theme the next quarter with a Mickey Mouse theme meeting. He had a gigantic seven-foot inflatable mouse to keep us company while we tried to listen to him speak with Mouseketeer ears on. I had a hard time taking My Stupid CEO seriously while he spoke with those ears on. He also splurged for a taco buffet, but we had to eat on Mickey Mouse plates.

My Stupid CEO wanted all of us to think outside the box for the next quarter. He figured the Disney theme would remind us that Disneyland was an original, creative, and innovative concept. I do agree that Disneyland was a state of the art concept. However, it's hard for us to think when we know that a creative kid with a lemonade stand is earning more than us. I don't even want to tell you what happened during the third-quarter meeting. All I can comment on is that we were forced to dress up as characters from Scooby Doo and walk around in public.

"My Stupid CEO wanted to know why there weren't air holes in condoms."

—Sidney S. Prasad

My Stupid CEO attempted to foster an environment where he expected all his employees to be friends outside of work. Working in a cutthroat sales environment, I had no desire to be seen with those mutants outside of work. I always had some well-rehearsed bullshit excuse when invited to a company shindig. My Stupid CEO and his wife, Anita Dyck, organized a company laser tag game one day. But to their regret, they didn't realize that half the organization was over age forty and morbidly fat. My colleagues weren't people you could picture running with laser tag guns zapping one another.

My Stupid CEO made another attempt at forcing everyone in our company to be friends. His ingenious idea to combat the socialization issue was to convert our parking lot into a bowling alley. After working fifty hours in a hostile work environment, no one was really keen on sticking around to bowl in a parking lot. He tried to bribe everyone with hot dogs and juice, which just reinforced his stupidity. Most of my colleagues would have stuck around if it was a proper barbecue with all the trimmings. We could go to the big box stores on Saturday morning and score free hot dogs and drinks. Plus, there would be no obligation to hang out with the freakshows that we worked with. I'm not sure if it was stupidity or ignorance on My Stupid CEO's part for not realizing that his employees didn't want to play with each other outside of work.

"My Stupid CEO was so dumb he thought Bill Gates was an outstanding Home Depot debt."

—Sidney S. Prasad

6 CHICKEN SHIT

I strongly believe the worst thing a parent can do is teach their kids to lie. Because when you teach your kids to lie for you, it eventually leads to them lying to you. For instance, many parents instruct their kids to tell telemarketers that their mom is asleep or their father got drafted to fight the War on Terror. Learning bad habits at a young age will develop a mature mind full of deceit and craftiness.

In my early days of selling, I used to manage a leather emporium, and I was constantly tied up in meetings and presentations. I had a very simple strategy to conquer the incoming calls that I couldn't get to. I simply told my employees to tell the caller that I was in the building but not available for an hour or so. I would always add on an extra fifteen minutes for a coffee and a quick shit-break. Ethically and spiritually, lying wasn't an option. Working in a public setting with showroom hours of 9:00 AM to 9:00 PM daily, it wouldn't be too difficult for a client to bust me if I were to lie about my presence. Once a businessman is caught lying, it makes it very difficult for his clients to trust him.

"My Stupid CEO tried to mug someone on an airplane."

—Sidney S. Prasad

Unfortunately, My Stupid CEO was a chronic, pathological liar. He refused to take any calls and we were instructed to transfer any callers to his voicemail. The only flexibility we would have is offering the client his email if they got sick of leaving him messages. I can't tell you how many countless people reported that My Stupid CEO wouldn't reply to his voice messages and emails.

I'm not sure what he was scared of in terms of responding to someone's messages. Before the "Do Not Call List" got created, the average American would receive about seven telemarketing calls daily. The majority of the population didn't hesitate to decline the offer or tell the telemarketer to go fuck themselves. So I really don't know what was up My Stupid CEO Izzy Cumming's ass.

As employees, when our superiors teach us to lie for them, they end up schooling us in how to lie to them. The office slut, Liz Bien, was always missing work to go to the abortion clinic. Her sad excuses were really lame. She convinced My Bipolar Manager that her brother ran over the lawnmower cord and got electrocuted. The sad thing was we were all fully aware that she lived in a subsidized housing apartment where the landlord mowed the lawn. Other chicks in my office would call in sick and then post pictures up on Facebook of them getting drunk at the hockey game the night before.

"My Stupid CEO put condoms on his ears to avoid hearing aids."

—Sidney S. Prasad

I inherited this one bitch named Ayma Moran from the previous sales executive that I replaced. Ayma Moran was the most hated client in our industry. In fact, all of our competitors refused to deliver to her office. Her company was a discount real estate firm that offered commissions below the one-percent mark. They leased the most awkward office, I guess to keep operating costs low. The building where their office was located was over a hundred years old. It was also considered a historical landmark. There was no elevator in that building, and the city bylaws didn't permit one to get built, so there was a hike of fifty-two steps to her third-floor headquarters.

Ayma Moran would place a pretty hefty order punctually every quarter. Whenever she would order, I would have to listen to a song and dance from the logistics manager, Ray Pist. Ray Pist would insist that I alter her invoice and increase her prices because of the hassle encountered by our delivery drivers. I refused, as increasing the prices would be against my personal code of ethics. One Wednesday afternoon, my phone rang two minutes before my lunch break. Ayma Moran kept me on the phone for two hours, ordering a bunch of shit. She never felt comfortable ordering online because she wasn't the sharpest tool in the shed. After fucking up my lunch reservations at the food court in the mall, I thanked her for her order and told her I would send a truck her way the following day.

"My Stupid CEO thought horseplay was something that happened at rodeos."

—Sidney S. Prasad

Ray Pist blew a gasket and told me that he refused to deliver to her unless I increased the prices on her invoice by thirty percent. My Bipolar Manager and My Stupid CEO were not in the office during Ray Pist's hissy fit. Because he was the only manager in the building, it was martial law, and I had to obediently listen to this loser's bullshit. Ray Pist put a gun to my head and made me call back Ayma Moran. I informed her that if he she didn't pay a thirty percent surcharge, we would cancel her order. Ayma Moran swore at me for a good hour and told me that I would never work in this town again unless she got her toilet paper delivered the next day. After the call, I went to the shitter and caught up with the NHL playoff highlights. While I was deciding whether I should bet against my city, Ayma Moran emailed My Stupid CEO a complaint letter about our conversation.

Ayma Moran's letter specifically stated that if she didn't get an email response or a phone call from My Stupid CEO, she would be forced to go to the media about his incompetence. My Stupid CEO shit his pants and was too chicken to respond to her. He pawned the duty off onto My Bipolar Manager, who escaped by telling him that he had to volunteer at a charity event. My Stupid CEO got one of his friends who had no clue about our industry to call her and mediate. Naturally, the idiot friend of My Stupid CEO gave into Ayma Moran's demands and gave her free next-day delivery.

Regardless of ethnicity, the average wedding consists of five hundred guests. Therefore, the average person knows about two hundred and fifty people. Companies can't afford to piss off their clientele because shit like this gets around really fast. My Stupid CEO told me that Ayma Moran was crazy and a cheapskate based on the discounted real estate brokerage that she worked for.

"My Stupid CEO thought Wite Out was a racial term."

— Sidney S. Prasad

I learned really fast that My Stupid CEO was a coward and too scared to be alone with any of his employees in the boardroom. Eileen Dover told me that in her seven years with the organization she had never been alone with My Stupid CEO. She even told me about an alcoholic that used to work in our warehouse. The piss-tank used to sip on a bottle of Jack Daniel's while he picked orders. Rather than fire the guy himself, My Stupid CEO got his wife to do it for him. If My Stupid CEO ever had a specific message or complaint to deliver to us, he would tell My Bipolar Manager to relay it to us. I felt like I was working for a mob boss who got his phone calls secondhand or something.

My Stupid CEO read a book one day that revolved around corporate restructuring. The author explained that in some cases, it's good to do a corporate sweep, fire all the employees, and start fresh. In some situations, I can adapt to that philosophy and support it. If one owns a company whose employees are ripping the company off blind, then by all means, do a clean out. However, it should be a gradual clean up. Certain key team members need to be replaced after an adequate replacement has been trained in their position, or the company could fall apart overnight.

"My Stupid CEO thought that the first class section of an airplane came with a teacher."

—Sidney S. Prasad

Hugh Jass was My Stupid CEO's best friend and a longtime trusted employee from the first day the company opened. Hugh Jass's role included acting as our CFO and our main I.T. expert. He knew all the mechanics of our company, including the ins-and-outs of our website. Based on some bullshit that My Stupid CEO read in a fortune cookie, he decided to fire Hugh Jass. Rather than take Hugh Jass in the boardroom and talk to him, man to man, My Stupid CEO Izzy Cumming took a complete different route. He hired a terminator named Horace Scope to do his dirty work for him. Horace Scope's brilliant plan was to clean out the entire contents of Hugh Jass's office and courier it to his house on Christmas Day. The package also included a termination letter and a final paycheck.

After Christmas, the company started to fall apart because My Stupid CEO didn't think about who was going to fill Hugh Jass's spot. Finding a replacement was crucial, considering that our company website was our bread and butter, and without an I.T. expert we were doomed to failure. My Stupid CEO cheaped out and hired an accounting student who had dropped out of school to take care of CFO duties. My Stupid CEO hired his old buddy Wayne Kerr to specialize in the I.T. aspect of the company. He even gave Wayne Kerr the title of vice president. Once again, another stupid mistake: hiring two people to do the job of one person.

Wayne Kerr's track record in the business world was horrendous. He successfully ran three companies into the ground and was bankrupt himself. He didn't know his ass from a hole in the ground.

"My Stupid CEO asked the hostess for potato chips."

—Sidney S. Prasad

Wayne Kerr clearly demonstrated the IQ of a six-year-old, but he had some street smarts. Within a month of his arrival, he realized that his hands would be full with the new international website issues, so he convinced My Stupid CEO to hire another vice president to pick up the slack between accounting and the I.T. department. Harry Cox got hired as our third vice president. He also was dumb as a doorknob. Harry Cox loved his BBC documentaries and based his whole life on whatever a reporter would post on the news. The sad thing with living one's life based on media recommendations is the constant fluctuation of opinions. One day, the media will report that having a glass of wine every day is hazardous to your health, and then the next day, they will say it's healthy.

Harry Cox got away with carrying his coffee around and observing the office. My Stupid CEO surely had a man-crush on him, because he let him get away with murder.

As time progressed, My Stupid CEO turned into even a bigger chicken shit. He pretty much handed the decision-making keys on a platter to Harry Cox and Wayne Kerr and merely hid behind them. Sadly, My Stupid CEO used to make bad jokes about Wayne Kerr and Harry Cox figuring out what duties they needed *him* to do.

As the company started going downhill, I attempted to schedule a meeting with My Stupid CEO to share some turnaround strategies, but he refused to be alone with me. I was told to speak to Harry Cox or Wayne Kerr, as they represented his interests—even though they had no fucking idea how our industry functioned.

"My Stupid CEO put clothes on his salad."

—Sidney S. Prasad

7 CHEAP TRICK

I personally have some of the cheapest lowlifes for relatives. One of my aunts used to rip off cutlery from the hospital cafeteria and used it in her home. Yet she failed to think about how many thousands of sick people have used those forks and knives. I've got an uncle who has Howard Johnson's and Holiday Inn towels throughout his multimillion dollar mansion. The lowest thing that I have seen was witnessing a relative go shopping in the lost and found at her child's school. Oh yes, and she drove away in her brand new Mercedes after looting the school.

By now, I'm quite sure that you have guessed that being a cheapskate was part of My Stupid CEO's psychological makeup. The writing was all over the walls, yet I never acknowledged the signs that My Stupid CEO was the most frugal schmuck in the world. Like this one time, there was a special party in honor of a truck driver's fifteen-year anniversary with the company. My Stupid CEO catered the party with four large pizzas and a thirty-pack of beer among forty people. I felt embarrassed for My Stupid CEO, and wasn't sure if it was a slight oversight or if he deliberately cheaped out. I didn't touch the booze that day because having one beer is like a fucking dick tease to me. It's sort of like getting all horny from a lap dance and not being able to do anything with the stripper.

"My Stupid CEO asked a pregnant woman her views on abortion."

—Sidney S. Prasad

My Stupid CEO was on a mission to expand the company's Facebook friend list. We all voted on having a thing called Facebook Friday, where we would randomly draw one of our Facebook friends to receive a special gift. This maneuver quadrupled our Facebook list within two months of instituting the program. However, My Stupid CEO really displayed his thriftiness by the prizes that he gave out. There were times when he would give a five-dollar box of chocolates, and then there were other occasions where he would give a gingerbread house kit in the middle of summer. I never saw a gift with a perceived value of more than fifteen dollars given out. My clients who won prizes expressed feelings of disappointment and anger.

Coming from a marketing background, I have a deep appreciation for cameras and advertising tools. Both our online and offline company catalogues had over one hundred thousand items listed in them. Any sane, savvy businessman would invest in a decent camera to capture the features and benefits of the products that they were advertising. My Stupid CEO relied on a one hundred dollar digital camera from back when President Clinton was running the country.

Speaking of cameras, My Stupid CEO decided to institute YouTube commercials and product review videos on our website to intrigue our clients. My Stupid CEO used a video camera that couldn't have been worth more than two hundred dollars. He didn't understand that when competing against big *Fortune 500* companies, the product images that we display would have to be on par with our competitors'.

"My Stupid CEO's favorite color was 'clear.'"

—Sidney S. Prasad

I mentioned earlier in this book that I never received that six-figure salary that I envisioned during business school. Reflecting on the *Business Week* salary surveys and the going rate for our industry, My Stupid CEO lowballed all of his employees. After my probationary period was over, I got to keep my job and the exact same salary that I began with. After completing my first year and being loyal, I got to keep my job at the same salary, again. After completing the second year, Harry Cox gave me a fifty-cent raise, a sweaty handshake, and a card with no money inside. Fuck, at least throw in a couple of lottery tickets or condoms or something. I told My Bipolar Manager that they could keep their raise because I was insulted. My Bipolar Manager convinced me that would rock the boat and bring myself onto My Stupid CEO's radar if I made that suggestion.

There was a major diarrhea issue in our company because My Stupid CEO got deals on almost-expired food. I never knew that soda pop had an expiry date till I worked for him. It wasn't economically feasible in my mind to feed employees bad shit because we spent half our shift in the shitter. If my ass could talk, it would have given My Stupid CEO shit for supplying rough, sandpaper-like, one-ply toilet paper. At least give us the luxury of having two-ply ass-wipe.

There was one positive factor about drinking his almost-expired and expired beverages. After a major weekend drinking binge, I'd have a free detox when I got to work on Monday. This would be the perfect time to mention that the washroom fan had been broken for over a decade and My Stupid CEO refused to fix it. Instead, he offered an air freshener bottle in an attempt to kill the smell.

"My Stupid CEO thought thieves ate hot meals."

—Sidney S. Prasad

Being a dot-com company whose sales are primarily generated online, one would be led to believe that the employees would be furnished with top-notch computers. The computers that we were supplied with resembled something from the early nineties. I was tempted to wear a leather jacket with an eight-ball on the back to go along with the theme. Harry Cox persuaded My Stupid CEO to invest in some decent computers. My Stupid CEO got a deal on all-in-one computers. The monitor, CD drive, and CPU were all in one unit. However, we received a memo to unplug our computers every night because one of them caught fire. Apparently, My Stupid CEO Izzy Cumming got a fly-by-night deal from a computer manufacturer that went bankrupt from the recall on its computer units.

I experienced a terrible car accident during my first year in the company where my SUV flipped over four times. My Stupid CEO sympathized by reminding me that I had no sick days and if I took time off to heal, I wouldn't get paid. Like Superman, I went back to work immediately after the accident. Since I had no benefits, I couldn't buy any of the drugs that my doctor prescribed to me. I found a solution by picking up some really cheap, raunchy tequila from the border. I would take a couple of shots every night and sleep on the floor until my back readjusted. I was hoping to get one of those cheap-ass computer-generated Get Well cards from my company to use as a dartboard, but I guess it wasn't in the budget.

"My Stupid CEO got his ass kicked in for telling 'yo mama' jokes at a family reunion."

—Sidney S. Prasad

On one occasion, My Stupid CEO rented out a private room of a two-star restaurant. Half of my colleagues didn't drive because they couldn't afford to operate their vehicles on what My Stupid CEO was paying them, while the other half just chanced it and drove with no car insurance. One guy even admitted to siphoning gas because he lived in his car and needed to use the heater during winter. My Bipolar Manager coordinated a carpool and bundled everyone together to get to the restaurant. Unfortunately, I had to share a car with My Bipolar Manager, and I would rather have hitchhiked to the restaurant.

When we arrived at the restaurant, we discovered that My Stupid CEO splurged on five appetizers for forty people. He expected us to feed off the snack trays like vultures fighting over a piece of bread. I am personally a germaphobe and can confirm that half of my coworkers don't wash their hands after taking a shit. While my colleagues raped the snack tray like it was their last supper, I sat in the corner with a glass of water. It's amazing how many people who don't wash their hands on a daily basis love to lick their fingers.

"My Stupid CEO said Wisconsin was cheesy."

—Sidney S. Prasad

My Bipolar Manager came up to me to inquire why I wasn't eating. I replied by telling him that I saw Gabe Oy scratching his balls at work, so that eliminated the nachos. Winnie Bago used her hands as Kleenex, and that eliminated the fried zucchini sticks and onion rings. The other two dishes had meat in them, and I was a vegan.

Quite frankly, even if I did eat meat, I wouldn't go near those two meat platters, anyways. That was because the office slut Liz Bien was doing something obscene with one of the warehouse guys during her lunch break and was snacking on them. God only knows what types of diseases she was hosting. So you figure My Stupid CEO would treat me to a vegetarian meal. Fuck, it would work in his favor, since most vegetarian dishes are like the cheapest thing on the menu.

My Stupid CEO overheard the conversation with My Bipolar Manager and didn't jump in to offer a solution. My Bipolar Manager end up treating me to dinner, which was really surprising, considering the guy knew that I hated his guts.

"If an employee can take a mental health day off, then can a bipolar manager take a mental health year off?"

—Sidney S. Prasad, *My Bipolar Manager*

My Stupid CEO promised free booze to anyone who attended the meeting. I went to the waitress and ordered some shitty Californian wine, but found out that I wasn't allowed to order it, because it was imported. She said that if I wanted wine, I was limited to some nasty Canadian wine in a box. I told her to get me a triple Grey Goose vodka with Red Bull. She declined me, and said that I was restricted to some domestic pissy vodka made in the Rocky Mountains. She also stated she couldn't serve me a triple because My Stupid CEO instructed her to give an "unlimited" two drinks per person. Fuck. I guess we all have different interpretations of the word "unlimited."

'The waitress also informed me I would personally have to pay for the Red Bull, because My Stupid CEO would only pay for fountain pop and Red Bull wasn't part of that deal. I would have to take a second mortgage on my cardboard house to pay for the Red Bull, so I took the vodka on ice.

"My Stupid CEO asked the bartender for the recipe for ice."

—Sidney S. Prasad

8 BAD DECISIONS

I don't know where to begin with the countless bad decisions that my team and I witnessed My Stupid CEO making. But let's start off with him not being an independent thinker. I have seen successful businessmen solely piggyback off the competition and mimic everything their competitors were doing. Bright men such as Henry Ford surrounded themselves with successful people who got the job done. But one of the mission-critical errors My Stupid CEO made was exclusively depending on his suit dummy executive team. The left half of his brain was dependent on Harry Cox and his BBC documentaries, while the right half was dependent on Wayne Kerr. If you are going to rely on expert advice, then make sure the so-called experts have verified successful track records. Otherwise, your company will have the rollercoaster ride of a lifetime.

Wayne Kerr manipulated My Stupid CEO into allowing him to mislead all of our clients. Wayne Kerr would basically pick random items on a daily basis and inflate the online prices without the clients' knowledge. The poor sales executives would get the shitty end of the stick and listen to the clients' bitch them out about price discrepancies between the offline and online catalogues. My Stupid CEO didn't see the big picture.

Wayne Kerr basically had to find a way to justify his presence in our company. So every week, he would come out looking like a hero when he would tell My Stupid CEO that he successfully ripped off ten thousand dollars from various clients by inflating the prices on them.

"My Stupid CEO thought Hamburger Helper was a McDonald's employee."

—Sidney S. Prasad

My Stupid CEO continued to give Wayne Kerr performance raises based on his criminal behavior. Meanwhile, the sales executives would be getting in butt-loads of shit from their clients, who were abandoning our company for price gouging them. This was really short-term gain and long-term pain. After about six months of looting our customers, our company sales were cut in half while profits continued to rise.

My Stupid CEO attempted to give us a wishy-washy motivational speech to turn things around. He basically wasted our time by telling us a story about a rocket-ship full of oranges that was going to another planet to set up a shop. He then said some of the oranges became rotten along the way because of their negativity, which was supposed to represent our sales team's attitude. The moral of the story was a backhanded threat that if the sales team didn't increase their sales, he would fire us.

Eventually, almost the entire sales department ended up leaving the company because they had had it with My Stupid CEO's shit. None of us could find a balance in our hostile work environment between My Stupid CEO and My Bipolar Manager. My Stupid CEO ignored complaints from the entire company that My Bipolar Manager wasn't mentally stable. He also never listened to my pleas that guy couldn't sell shit to a toilet paper factory.

One day, I purposely sent out My Bipolar Manager Iman S. Hole and My Stupid CEO to represent me in a sales meeting. Prior to the meeting, My Bipolar Manager admitted to My Stupid CEO that he was nervous and didn't know how to conduct himself in a presentation. That should have indicated that he wasn't qualified for his position.

"My Stupid CEO tried to hire a realtor from the Home Shopping Network."

—Sidney S. Prasad

My Bipolar Manager told me that My Stupid CEO didn't even do a reference check on him when he hired him off the street. Basically, any of our competitors could have disguised themselves as an applicant for a sales manager position. Then, once our competitors had gained access to our database, they could have totally sabotaged the company. They would know our costs and be able to undercut our prices. The competition would also be able to export our client list to their database. It would only make sense to do a rigorous background investigation on the individual who was going to guard the company's sales, right?

After speaking to all my colleagues in various departments, all of us agreed that we were collectively underpaid. My Stupid CEO made the bad decision of being too greedy. In my mind, a CEO shouldn't vocalize the sales and profit figures to the entire company unless its employees are fairly compensated. It killed me inside knowing that for every million dollars in sales I brought to the company, three hundred and fifty thousand dollars in profit would be deposited into My Stupid CEO's mattress. Every night when I'd be eating my Kraft Dinner, I would be swearing in my head at that asshole, "Give me a fucking raise so I can eat something different!" There are some people who can never be rich regardless of how much money they hoard in their lifetime.

"My Stupid CEO tried to buy a plasma TV using a *TV Guide*."

—Sidney S. Prasad

From what I understand, anyone who works in the public eye would be fired on the spot for cursing at a customer, because all customers are protected by "the customer is always right" bullshit. There was this one redneck named Gabe Oy that worked in our warehouse. This little fucker was always on the rag and pissed off about something. Based on his performance and attitude at being the world's biggest asshole, My Stupid CEO promoted him to a delivery driver position. Gabe Oy had a lot of no-show deliveries and got away with taking a week to do a next-day delivery. All the sales executives carried his ass and listened to the customers bitch about running out of toilet paper and wiping their asses on the wall because their delivery was days overdue.

"I noticed on your online dating profile under the subject heading: personality, you put multiple."

—Sidney S. Prasad, *My Bipolar Manager*

One of my clients, Barb Aye, was expecting a delivery one afternoon, so she put a sign on her front door. The sign explained that she would be across the street grabbing coffee for five minutes and for the driver to wait for her in case he showed up while she was absent. As she was leaving the Starbucks, she saw Gabe Oy pulling out of her office driveway. She politely apologized for missing him and wanted her supplies. He ripped a strip off her and cursed in many four-letter words, then made the poor girl unload the shit by herself.

When she called to complain to me, I immediately transferred her to Wayne Kerr, our vice president. I was confident that we would rid ourselves of this cancerous redneck and he would be fired on the spot. My Stupid CEO allowed Gabe Oy to keep his job. He just instructed the guy to work in the warehouse for a few days because he thought the pressure of the traffic was getting to him. I was flabbergasted and astonished that My Stupid CEO let him get away with this terrible act.

"My Stupid CEO thought Dairy Queen was a porn star."

—Sidney S. Prasad

9 STUPIDITY IS A HABIT

I believe that stupidity is a bad habit people develop over the course of time and not an inherited trait. The history books are filled with examples of astute men and women who had dumb children with pedestrian lifestyles. Equally, there are many tales of children who had alcoholic, destitute, and mindless parents, and they aspired to high levels of success. There are also people who have fluctuating intelligence, and periodically make comebacks and celebrate their successes.

I wish I could pinpoint the contributing factors which lead to the downfall of people's intelligence. Some may speculate that spending too much time watching television can make one's mind go to mush. Addiction to fatty foods, alcoholic beverages, and drugs can also take a person down a bad path and steer their mind off their goals. Laziness and having an idle mind can also affect successful decision making, in my opinion.

"I asked My Bipolar Manager, how many mood rings has he broken in the last five minutes?"

—Sidney Prasad, *My Bipolar Manager*

In My Stupid CEO's case, he appeared to be overly spontaneous and live only for the moment. If he read something in a book or heard something in a seminar, he would want to test it out immediately. There is nothing wrong with experimenting; however, it's extremely important to weigh the pros and cons before executing your moves, especially when they affect a database of ten thousand clients and several employees. There are a lot of loose cannons in the business world who have sunk an entire company with just one stupid bold move.

"My Stupid CEO tried to give Webster back his dictionary."

—Sidney S. Prasad

You are a product of your environment and should carefully guard your mind against those you surround yourself with. There are many homes in the ghetto whose family members are fifth-generation welfare recipients. The conversation around the dinner table always revolved around receiving their welfare check. My Stupid CEO made a crucial error in aligning his mind with his executive suit dummy team. Not only did they contribute to our company's failure, they also made My Stupid CEO into even a looser cannon. All the vice presidents that he hired had no experience in our industry, which should have disqualified them from getting hired.

Life coaching and corporate coaching have been on the rise in the last couple of decades. My Stupid CEO hired an acquaintance of his named Ida Hoe to coach him in turning around his business. I immediately creeped on his friend's LinkedIn profile and discovered she wasn't qualified to manage a broom closet. This chick basically made a career of managing retail lingerie stores, and all of a sudden was a turnaround expert.

My Stupid CEO started relying on this ex-underwear saleswoman's advice on how to run his company. She convinced him to plant a mole amongst the staff and find out who was insubordinate. To make a long story short, this mole increased the tension and hostility inside the company when it was announced that she was a spy. Our company continued to spiral downhill while Ida Hoe and her mole earned a few fast bucks with their crappy corporate coaching. The entire company wished that My Stupid CEO would locate his brain, take the shrink-wrap off and use it, rather than take outside advice on how to wipe his ass.

"My Stupid CEO tried to buy a brand new antique."

—Sidney S. Prasad

In the biographies and life stories of many successful men and women, it's common that they disclose that "success is a habit." The habit of going to bed early, the habit of effectively managing time, the habit of research and developing the mind. It takes twenty-one days to form a habit and just three days to break it. For example, a person might have an exercise routine of going to the gym six days a week and taking one day off. But if all of a sudden they get around a go-nowhere group and start missing a few days, the effects can be detrimental. Rapid weight gain begins, followed by a cycle of laziness, and eventually he or she ends up not working out for an extended period.

My Stupid CEO developed the bad habit of ignoring his frontline staff and wouldn't acknowledge them at times. I attempted to explain to him the Japanese management model of suggestion. I emailed him examples of successful Japanese companies who mandated that all their employees give a minimum of one suggestion per shift. I urged him to create a suggestion box for his employees to contribute their ideas. My justification was that on the front line, so much information is expressed to us that can have an impact on the company, both positive and negative. This was a very simple request on my part that My Stupid CEO ignored.

"My Stupid CEO tossed a quarter in a well and thought it was welfare."

—Sidney S. Prasad

Maybe it was selective hearing, but My Stupid CEO did adopt one of my ideas, with which I felt I shot myself in the foot. I told him about how I used to teach my employees to self-motivate themselves. This involved using a picture of any sort of goal they had. For example, if someone's goal was to purchase a fifteen-hundred dollar handbag, I would have them get a picture of that handbag and hang it by their workspace. Each time the employee would be in the middle of speaking to a client, they could reflect on the picture. The visual image would remind the employee to close the sale, so they could buy the handbag.

My Stupid CEO told the entire sales team to put pictures of their goals on their cubicle walls. Here's where I screwed myself: I put a picture of a house and a Jeep. My Stupid CEO stole my dream and purchased that exact Jeep and flaunted it in my face. The house that was on my vision board was in this resort town a few hours away. My Stupid CEO made a special trip out shortly after, and the rumor was that he bought a weekend home there. I should have put a picture of a piece of shit on a plate.

"My Stupid CEO stayed up all night to study for a drug test."

—Sidney S. Prasad

10 PENNY FOR YOUR THOUGHTS

Throughout the course of this book, you have learned about some dense moves made by My Stupid CEO. At times, it appeared that he lacked common sense and good decision making skills. There are many questions that I am sure that are lingering in your mind, such as, "How did a man this stupid get into the executive suite?" Some things in life appear completely different when you get up close and personal with them. A lot of celebrities act in a different manner off-camera and treat their fans like poop. Their off-camera personalities would be polar opposites to the characters they portray on the big screen.

I am not in any way attempting to deter prospective business students from entering the corporate world. But I am trying to convey the message that there are unexpected surprises in the business environment. I did my homework and carefully researched the company's background and My Stupid CEO's track record. There were countless local newspapers and business magazines that boasted about his success. Never in my wildest dreams had I expected the guy to be a complete phony and an imbecile, as opposed to what was advertised in the mainstream media.

"My Stupid CEO attempted to cheat on a survey."

—Sidney S. Prasad

America is a ladder, and we all must decide when to get on and when to jump off. There are tales of people who started off as chauffeurs for big businessmen and eventually became vice presidents of the organization. Contrariwise, there are people who remain in the same occupational title for the duration of their career. One man's resume can state that he has ten years' experience in a given field, while another man can honestly admit that he has one year's experience, ten times over. Life is all about choices, but sometimes we get ourselves into situations where we have no control whatsoever.

Most people in my shoes would have thrown in the towel when they discovered their so-called mentor was dumber than a sixth grader. I decided to tough it out and learn about myself with this experience. I never considered myself naïve, but I wouldn't be surprised hearing that accusation. The justification for someone to accuse me of naïveté would be based on my failing to recognize that My Stupid CEO had no brain. Within the first couple of months, I realized he was lacking something in his ability to conduct business and his success was a fluke. Working for him really forced me to develop a new philosophy and perception of life. I developed the habit of questioning the popular opinion and popular vote. This also led me to formulate the habit of thinking outside the box.

"My Stupid CEO thought it was impossible to eat Frosted Flakes on a hot day."

—Sidney S. Prasad

My advice for anyone contemplating getting into the business world is to go in with an open mind. There are many factors that alter the dynamics of a successful business overnight: the weather, stock market fluctuations, commodity prices, world events, and the men and women at the top of the corporate pyramid. Do your homework like I did, and weigh the pros and cons. However, always have a Plan B in case you discover you have inherited a Stupid CEO. Some people may choose to ride it out, while others may just jump ship immediately. The choice is essentially yours, as you are in the driver's seat with full control of your destiny.

"My Stupid CEO thought the sky was a sunroof."

—Sidney S. Prasad

My Stupid CEO continues to hold onto his dream of being the number-one online supplier of janitorial supplies. Even though sales have drastically declined, reporters are still writing positive stories about My Stupid CEO. My Stupid CEO was also approached to contend to be among the top fifty employers in my state, regardless of all the chaos going on. If there was ever such thing as the Seven Corporate Wonders of the World, I am sure he would have the number-one spot.

The majority of my colleagues jumped ship, and the company lost over two-thirds of its employees. My opponent was My Bipolar Manager, who was even more of a bigger piece of work. You can learn all about him in a book called *My Bipolar Manager*. I eventually did leave the company after a huge victory over My Bipolar Manager. The one-third of employees who remained in the company thought they were victims of fate. Karmically, the remaining employees thought they were paying for something they did at another point in time during their working careers.

Life is what we make it to be. One may bitch about the glass being half-empty, while another will see it as a cue to order another round. Working for My Stupid CEO got me to wake up and smell the killer Kool-Aid. If he had never come into my life, I might have continued respecting the business elite and not question how they obtained their power and wealth. The future holds a mysterious question: What would happen the day My Stupid CEO started using his brain?

For those of you interested in learning about the biggest walking corporate disaster, I highly recommend you read *My Bipolar Manager.*

ABOUT THE AUTHOR

Sidney S. Prasad is an author on a quest to make the world laugh. His work is focused on entertaining people with his dry-humored novels. Sidney S. Prasad personally believes laughter is the best cure for all of life's ups and downs.

Some other humorous books written by Sidney S. Prasad include:

How To Piss Off A Telemarketer,
How To Piss Off A Salesman
My Bipolar Manager,
Don't Ask Dumb Questions!,
Corny Names & Stupid Places,
Misfortune Cookies,
How To Irritate A Telemarketer
Plenty Of Freaks: Are You Sold On Online Dating?
Plenty Of Freaks: Worst Online Dating Mistakes
Plenty Of Freaks: Is Dating Legalized Prostitution?
and
Telemarketer's Revenge: The Customer Is Always Wrong, Bitch!